60 DAYS TO RICHES

PRACTICAL STRATEGIES TO BUILDING LASTING SUCCESS

ABBY FALOY

CONTENTS

Title Page

Copyright

INTRODUCTION 1

CHAPTER ONE 3

CHAPTER TWO 15

CHAPTER THREE 22

CHAPTER FOUR 28

CHAPTER FIVE 35

INTRODUCTION

60 Days to Riches is a program meant to assist individuals to reach their financial objectives in a short amount of time. This book is built on the notion that with the correct mentality, tools, and methods, anyone can attain financial success in a very short length of time.

The challenge is separated into three primary phases: defining financial objectives and targets, devising a plan of action, and implementing and measuring success. Each step is meant to help individuals construct a firm foundation for success, generate momentum, and achieve their financial objectives within 60 days.

In the first part, individuals will be urged to define clear and precise financial goals and targets.

This involves determining the amount of money they would like to earn or save, the timeframe within which they would like to reach their goals, and the particular activities they need to take to attain them. The focus will be on developing SMART (specific, measurable, attainable, relevant, and time-bound) objectives that correspond with their own beliefs and priorities.

In the second phase, individuals will build a plan of action to attain their financial goals. This involves defining the resources they require, the particular tasks they need to take, and the timescale for completion. The plan of action will be broken down into smaller, achievable stages, and individuals will be urged to prioritize their activities based on what is most essential and what will have the largest influence on their financial success.

In the third and final phase, individuals will implement their plan of action and track their success. This involves monitoring their income and spending, keeping track of their savings, and making adjustments as appropriate. You are encouraged to stay focused and disciplined and to enjoy your victories along the way.
The 60 Days to Riches Challenge is not a get-rich-quick scam. Rather, it is a program designed to help individuals achieve their financial goals through hard work, discipline, and a commitment to success.

This book emphasizes the importance of setting clear goals, creating a plan of action, and taking consistent, focused action to achieve success. It is suitable for individuals at any stage of their financial journey, whether they are just starting or looking to take their finances to the next level.

In conclusion, "60 Days to Riches" presents an exciting opportunity for individuals to achieve their financial goals and transform their lives. By a mix of goal-setting, planning, and persistent action, participants will be able to develop a strong foundation for success and attain their financial ambitions within a short timeframe. Whether you are wanting to make more money, save for a significant purchase, or just take charge of your finances, the 60 Days to Riches Challenge may help you reach your objectives and realize your full potential.

CHAPTER ONE

LAYING THE FOUNDATION FOR SUCCESS

Building the foundation for success is a vital step toward accomplishing one's objectives and aspirations. Whether in personal or professional life, a firm foundation establishes the platform for development and success. In this book, we will review the main parts of developing a solid foundation for success, including defining objectives and priorities, having a strong mentality, and forming strong habits.

The first step in creating the basis for success is identifying clear objectives and priorities. Without precise objectives and priorities, it's impossible to build a strategy for success. Establishing objectives helps to develop concentration, motivation, and a feeling of direction. Objectives should be explicit, quantifiable, attainable, meaningful, and time-bound. These should match one's beliefs and priorities and be broken down into smaller, doable stages. For example, a financial goal may be saving $10,000 in six months, broken down into saving $1,667 every month. A health goal may be to lose 20 pounds in three months, broken down into dropping 1-2 pounds every week. Establishing defined objectives and priorities establishes a roadmap for success and helps to stay focused on what is vital.

The next stage in setting the basis for success is developing a strong mentality. A strong mentality is vital for attaining success. It's crucial to create a growth mindset, which is defined by a conviction that talents and intellect can be developed through devotion and hard effort. A growth mindset helps to promote resilience, flexibility, and a willingness to accept changes. To develop a growth mindset, it's important to embrace challenges, learn from failures, seek feedback, and persist in the face of obstacles. Positive self-talk, visualization, and mindfulness are other useful approaches for creating a strong mentality.

Building strong habits is also a key element in laying the foundation for success. Habits are behaviors that are repeated regularly and tend to occur subconsciously. Habits play a significant role in achieving success because they help to automate positive behaviors and reduce decision fatigue. Building strong habits requires consistency, discipline, and accountability. To build strong habits, it's important to start small and gradually increase the difficulty.

It's also important to identify triggers and cues that can help to reinforce positive behaviors. For example, a habit of exercising regularly could be reinforced by laying out workout clothes the night before or by setting a reminder on a smartphone.

In addition to setting goals, developing a strong mindset, and building strong habits, there are several other key elements of laying the foundation for success. These include:

Building strong relationships: Success is not achieved

in isolation. Building strong relationships with family, friends, mentors, and colleagues can provide support, guidance, and networking opportunities. Strong relationships are built on trust, respect, and mutual support.

Constant learning: Achievement demands ongoing learning and growth. It's crucial to be interested, seek out new information and experiences, and embrace lifelong learning. Reading, attending seminars and workshops, and networking are all great strategies to continue learning and improving.

Time management: Time is a valuable resource and managing it correctly is vital for attaining success. It's crucial to prioritize duties, remove distractions, and concentrate on high-value activities. Time management approaches such as the Pomodoro Technique, time blocking, and delegating may assist to improve productivity and decrease wasted time.

Financial management: Financial stability is a crucial part of success. Handling money efficiently entails developing a budget, limiting debt, saving for the future, and investing properly. Money management abilities may be strengthened by education, getting assistance from financial specialists, and creating solid money habits.

Self-care: Achievement demands physical and mental well-being. It's crucial to emphasize self-care activities such as exercise, a good diet, meditation, and spending time with loved ones. Taking care of oneself guarantees that energy and attention are maintained, lowering the danger.

Setting Financial Goals and Targets

Financial objectives are the long-term, short-term, and intermediate plans you have for your money. The finest financial goals match your beliefs and personal aspirations. Not to be mistaken with a budget or financial plan, financial objectives are defined and verifiable milestones that, when completed, get you closer to your ideal future.

Establishing suitable financial objectives needs a rather high degree of financial understanding. It's crucial to grasp the fundamentals of money, including how to construct a budget, the way taxes operate, the difference between kinds of investments, and several other personal finance subjects that affect your finances.

If you feel ill-equipped to make financial choices on your own and understand you need to increase your financial literacy, add this to your financial objectives today since this is the basis from which you will construct the goals that will support your whole financial future.

Your financial objectives are the particular monetary quantities you are committed to earning that will enable you to accomplish your vision for your life. Like with any objective, financial goals should be connected with your long-term intentions, whether these ambitions involve putting children through school, sustaining a specific retirement lifestyle, or paying off and keeping out of debt.

Excellent financial objectives are detailed. Generic objectives such as "raise my credit score" are unlikely to motivate you to attain them for a variety of reasons.

First, the purpose is vague. What is your current credit score? How high can you hope to increase your score in a particular time frame?

Even if you wrote down this goal and reviewed it every day, you would likely struggle to figure out where to start, and you wouldn't know when you'd achieved it.

Second, until you know why you want to improve your credit score — that is, the result you're looking for by improving your score — you won't feel a feeling of urgency to attain it. Maybe you read somewhere that you should have a credit score of 750, but you don't know why it matters. What's the advantage to you?

Although boosting your credit score is a reasonable objective for those with scores that lie in the 680 area, experts suggest that there is a point of diminishing returns after you achieve a credit score of 760. The question then becomes whether this goal is relevant to your current financial plan and status.

This is why you need SMART financial objectives.

SMART objectives are characterized by the following characteristics:

Specific
Measurable
Attainable

Relevant
Time-bound

If you adjusted the objective of "raising your credit score" to "improve my 680 credit score by 25 points over the next 12 months," you would have a SMART goal that could be monitored and quantified. The capacity to monitor this objective considerably boosts your chances of attaining it.

Your Objectives and Your Budget Go Hand-in-Hand
Establishing a reasonable budget and adhering to it is a good financial goal in itself. Without a budget, you will fail in your attempts to attain your objectives.

Money management and financial planning depend on excellent budgeting abilities. Your financial objectives are a component of your total financial plan, and your budget enables you to analyze your plan and change as required to attain your goals.

Much as great athletes maintain thorough records of their workouts and victories to gain perspective and monitor their growth, you can use your budget to examine your financial achievements and failures and discover any parts of your plan that may need to be altered.

Your budget will also provide you with a sense of control over your financial condition and the courage to endure in the face of financial misfortune.

Another frequently neglected advantage of a budget is its utility as a communication tool. Maybe you and your spouse are not seeing eye-to-eye in bits. Or maybe your kids believe money grows on trees, as the saying goes.

The ability to give concrete evidence of the family's spending patterns and how they are damaging everyone's objectives might bolster your case for having to cut down on take-out or putting a particular amount of money in the college fund every month.

The three categories of financial objectives are long-term (more than 10 years), mid-term (three to 10 years), and short-term (less than three years) (less than three years).

It's good to look at your financial objectives — not simply your assets — as either long-term, mid-term (or intermediate), or short-term.

Just as defining time frames for your investments will help you to strategize effectively, having clear, realistic periods for the rest of your financial objectives will better equip you to plan the measures you need to take to get closer to each one.

Long-Term Objectives
Long-term objectives, such as assuring financial stability in retirement or paying off your home, are farther off on the horizon. Your long-term financial goals often include several short-term or mid-term goals. It's usually a good idea to break down major objectives into smaller, more urgent ones.

Short-Term Goals
In addition to smaller, more narrowly focused goals that contribute to your long-term goals, you may also want

to set short-term goals for things you'd like to afford shortly, such as a bathroom renovation or a trip to France. Notice that our example here is specific. There's a reason behind this.

We need to give our financial goals specific, exciting names that conjure up images and feelings that thrill us.

The strength of financial psychology to help you reach your objectives is largely in the way it helps you to imagine the future and what success will look like. This applies to all of your financial objectives, not just your short-term ones.

Mid-term Objectives
Mid-term, or intermediate, objectives may involve initiatives such as saving the premium payment for an annuity that will give you lifetime income, boosting your credit score, or getting the funds to start your own company.

You may wish to research strategies to earn passive income or engage a financial expert to assist you to plan your retirement. Each of these examples of mid-term financial objectives has a period of three to ten years and is eventually a stepping stone to a greater goal.

Examples of various sorts of financial objectives include:

- Increase your financial literacy
- Make a budget
- Save for retirement and other long-term goals
- Save for short-term and mid-term plans

- Pay off debt
- Build excellent credit
- Earn more money
- Build an estate plan
-

Putting out clear, realistic financial objectives can help you attain them. Research suggests that those who write their objectives in paper and review them periodically have a greater probability of reaching them. This technique works as successfully for CEOs as it does for Olympic athletes, and it can work for you, no matter what sort of financial objectives you establish.

The physical character of detailed, written financial objectives makes them simpler to monitor, and the progress you make toward your short-term goals will keep you motivated to attain your intermediate and long-term goals, too.

The simple process of assessing your financial objectives and balancing your actions against your budget and priorities can enhance the probability that you will remain on track, sometimes sacrificing a night out or the newest generation of that tech item everyone else is charging to their credit cards.

Another — sometimes overlooked — advantage of establishing financial objectives is the reduction in stress and worry you'll feel when you confront your financial realities head-on.

Addressing personal stresses, the percentage of individuals who highlighted money as a cause of stress

(65%) was up in June (61%) and February (57%) in 2021. And in August 2022, it was revealed that Americans averaged $5,589 in credit card debt in 2022.

Consider the sensation of freedom in knowing that you're not among the 64 million debt-laden Americans, and let it drive you toward your objectives.

Strategies for Establishing Achievable Financial Objectives

Your financial objectives are unique to you. They are an extension of your values, of what's genuinely most important to you. You may discover that certain objectives are simpler to attain than others.

Maybe you're more driven to save money for traveling than for decorating your house. Your vision for your future should guide you as you establish your financial objectives.
It's impossible to get motivated toward your financial objectives if you don't relate your goal to the things you're most passionate about.

Ideas for leveraging financial psychology to attain your objectives include:

- Envision your ideal life and establish financial objectives that match your image.
- Give your objectives titles that create enthusiasm and drive.
- Time-stamp your objectives (a concept of SMART goals).
- Develop visual representations to help you

envision your objectives.

- Automate your success.

This final suggestion may have a major influence on your success. Automating as many of the tasks required in working toward your financial objectives might lessen the notion that you're doing without — or doing with less. And thankfully, there is a myriad of solutions accessible to help automate and monitor your financial objectives.

From direct deposits to savings accounts and autopay choices for credit cards to budgeting tools that connect to your accounts and update in real-time, you have resources for practically every sort of financial objective at your fingertips.

Some are free, some are subscription-based, and the perks and features differ. You'll have to evaluate these resources based on your objectives to decide if the benefit is worth the cost or, just as importantly, the time you'll have to invest to set them up and learn how to use them.

As with any tool, these software applications can't do everything for you. You'll need to regularly monitor your transactions and accounts and be aware of app settings and notifications to ensure everything is working the way you expect it to.
Keep in mind that any form of automation can throw off your budget if you don't track all transactions carefully.

In addition to online banking and automatic bill pay,

your bank may generate free spending reports, charts, and other visual data on its website that you can export to a spreadsheet or budgeting worksheet.

Finally, Do not wait, the time will never be 'just right.' Start where you stand, and work with whatever tools you may have at your command, and better tools will be found as you go along."

CHAPTER TWO

GENERATING QUICK CASH

Selling Unwanted Items and Decluttering

Selling old stuff and decluttering may be an efficient method to not only clear up space in your house but also make some additional cash. It is a procedure that includes identifying objects that are no longer required or utilized, assessing their worth, and then selling them via different channels.

The initial stage in the procedure is to identify goods that are no longer required or utilized. This may be done by looking through your stuff, room by room, and establishing a list of objects that are no longer providing a function. This may include clothes that no longer fit, appliances that have been replaced, and home décor that is no longer in vogue or no longer reflects your taste.

After you have selected objects that you no longer need or use, the following step is to assess their worth. This may be done via research on internet markets such as eBay or Amazon, or by consulting with a professional appraiser. It is crucial to precisely establish the worth of each item to ensure that you are pricing it effectively and not selling it for too little or too much.

After you have evaluated the worth of your products, the following step is to decide on the best channel for selling them. There is an aaansnannaaanmulaanitude of possibilities accessible, including internet marketplaces, local ads, garage sales, and consignment stores. Each channel has its benefits and downsides, and it is crucial to evaluate aspects such as convenience, costs, and time to sell before making a selection.

Internet marketplaces such as eBay and Amazon may be simple and effective methods to sell unwanted products. They provide a big audience of prospective consumers and the chance to contact buyers from all around the globe. Yet, they may also charge fees for listing and selling products and need some work to establish an efficient listing.

Local ads such as Craigslist or Facebook Marketplace may also be a fantastic choice for selling unused stuff. They are generally free to use and enable you to sell stuff fast and simply to local purchasers. But, they may also force you to meet with purchasers in person, which may be cumbersome or even risky.

Garage sales are another common alternative for selling unwanted stuff. They enable you to sell many things at once and maybe a pleasant and sociable way to declutter. Nevertheless, they need some work to arrange and may not be efficient in selling higher-value products.

Consignment stores may be a fantastic choice for selling higher-value things such as designer apparel or furnishings. They enable you to sell products on consignment, meaning that you earn a portion of the selling price when the item is sold. Yet, they may force you to wait for your item to sell and may charge a commission fee.

Regardless of the channel you use, it is necessary to build a good listing for your products. This may entail taking clear and thorough images, creating a convincing description, and pricing the item accordingly. You should also be prepared to bargain with prospective purchasers and reply to inquiries or concerns in a timely way.

Selling unwanted stuff and decluttering may be a pleasant and successful activity. It not only helps you to clear up space in your house but also makes some additional cash. By following these procedures and carefully examining your alternatives, you may effectively sell unwanted stuff and clear your house.

Taking Advantage of Side Hustles and Gig Economy

The gig economy has opened up a world of options for individuals to make additional cash outside of their usual occupations. Side hustles, or part-time work that may be done in addition to your primary source of income, have grown more popular as individuals explore for methods to supplement their incomes or follow their hobbies.

Initially, it is vital to determine your talents and hobbies. This can help you identify what sorts of side hustles or employment might be a suitable match for you. For example, if you are excellent in writing or graphic design, you may want to pursue freelancing in these fields. If you like driving and meeting new people, driving for ride-sharing services like Uber or Lyft might be a wonderful alternative.

After you have selected your talents and
interests, the following step is to study the available
options. Thereisaultitude of platforms and services
that provide side hustles and jobs, such as Upwork,
TaskRabbit, and Fiverr. These platforms enable you to
build a profile, promote your talents and expertise, and
interact with possible clients or consumers.
It is crucial to thoroughly check the terms and
conditions of each site to understand the costs, payment
methods, and expectations.

Some platforms may charge a commission fee for each
work you complete, while others may require you to bid
on contracts or establish your pricing. It is crucial to
pick a platform that corresponds with your aims and
expectations.

Another alternative for side hustles and employment is
to create your own company. This may entail selling
things or services online, having a blog or YouTube
channel, or launching a small company in your local
neighborhood. Establishing your own company enables
you to have more control over your money and schedule,
but also entails more work and risk.
Regardless of the platform or approach you use, it is
crucial to establish realistic objectives and expectations
for your side hustle or work. It may take time to build up
a customer base or establish oneself in a certain field, so
it is crucial to be patient and persistent.

In addition to the cash rewards of side hustles and

jobs, they may also give opportunities for personal growth and development. They enable you to explore new hobbies and abilities, meet new people, and obtain useful experience in diverse areas. They may also give a feeling of purpose and satisfaction outside of your usual employment.

Yet, it is crucial to balance your side hustle or gig with your other responsibilities, such as your primary work, family, and personal leisure. Burnout and weariness may be prevalent in the gig economy, so it is crucial to emphasize self-care and establish limits.

In conclusion, taking advantage of side hustles and the gig economy may be a terrific way to enhance your income and explore new options. By recognizing your talents and interests, investigating relevant possibilities, and establishing reasonable objectives and expectations, you may effectively navigate the world of side hustles and jobs. Just remember to emphasize self-care and balance your obligations to prevent burnout.

Tapping into the Sharing Economy

The sharing economy has become a popular option for people to make additional money, as well as for consumers to access products and services more inexpensively and conveniently. This economic model is built on the principle of sharing resources, whether it be a vehicle, lodging, or even a meal.

One of the most common methods to engage in the sharing economy is by renting out your house or assets. This may include renting out a spare room on Airbnb, renting out a vehicle on Turo, or renting out your parking spot on JustPark. By doing so, you may generate additional cash from resources that you already have.

It is crucial to recognize the risks and obligations connected with renting out your house or assets. Make sure you properly investigate and understand the terms and conditions of the site you are using, as well as any local laws or regulations that may apply. Moreover, make sure you have appropriate insurance coverage to protect yourself in the case of any accidents or losses.

Another option to get into the sharing economy is by giving services on sites such as TaskRabbit or Thumbtack. These platforms enable you to provide your talents and services to individuals in your local community, whether it be cleaning, dog walking, or handyman services. By selling your services via these channels, you may engage with new customers and expand your reputation and client base.

It is crucial to establish appropriate charges for your services and verify that you are offering value to your consumers. Excellent customer service and communication skills are also vital to guarantee that you obtain great evaluations and referrals, which may help you develop your company.

The sharing economy also provides chances to engage in the collaborative consumption of goods and services. For example, instead of owning a car, you can use a car-sharing service like Zipcar or Car2Go. Instead of buying new clothes, you can rent clothes through services like Rent the Runway or Le Tote. By participating in collaborative consumption, you can save money on goods and services that you may only need temporarily.

The sharing economy also offers opportunities for peer-to-peer lending and investing. This includes platforms like LendingClub, where individuals can invest in personal loans, or Fundrise, where individuals can invest in real estate projects. By participating in peer-to-peer lending and investing, you can earn passive income and diversify your investment portfolio.

The sharing economy offers a variety of opportunities to earn extra income and access goods and services more affordably and conveniently. By renting out your property or assets, offering your services, participating in collaborative consumption, and investing in peer-to-peer platforms, you can tap into the benefits of the sharing economy. However, it is important to understand the risks and liabilities associated with these activities and to take appropriate precautions to protect yourself and your assets.

CHAPTER THREE

INVESTING FOR RAPID RETURNS

Understanding the Basics of Investing

Investment is the act of allocating resources (typically money) with the hope of earning a return in the future. There are many various investment possibilities accessible, including stocks, bonds, real estate, and mutual funds. In this essay, we will explore the fundamentals of investing and how to get started.

The first step in investing is to identify financial objectives. This might involve saving for retirement, a down payment on a property, or a child's education. After you have determined your goals, you can start to build an investing plan that matches your objectives.

The next stage is to establish your risk tolerance. Risk tolerance refers to your capacity to absorb probable losses in your investment portfolio. If you are okay with taking on greater risk, you may wish to invest in higher-risk, higher-return assets like stocks. But, if you are risk-averse, you may choose to concentrate on lower-risk products like bonds.

After you have identified your risk tolerance, you may start to study alternative investing possibilities.

Equities are a popular investment choice since they provide the potential for significant profits but also come with increased risks. Bonds, on the other hand, are typically regarded as a lower-risk investment alternative but give smaller yields.

Real estate is another investment choice that may bring both income and long-term gain. Investing in a rental property or acquiring a property to flip may be a rewarding financial option. But, real estate investments need a large amount of cash and may be more difficult than other investing possibilities.

Mutual funds and exchange-traded funds (ETFs) are other popular investing choices. These investment vehicles enable you to invest in a diverse portfolio of stocks and bonds, which may assist to decrease risk. They are also often managed by professional investors, which might be a benefit for people who are new to investing.

Regardless of the investment strategy you select, it is crucial to maintain a long-term view. Investing is not a get-rich-quick plan, and it takes time for assets to develop and provide profits. It is also vital to constantly examine and adjust your portfolio to ensure that it stays aligned with your financial objectives and risk tolerance.

Investment is a vital aspect of developing wealth and accomplishing financial objectives. By learning the foundations of investing, identifying financial goals, evaluating your risk tolerance, and investigating various investment possibilities, you can design an investment plan that corresponds with your objectives. Remember to keep a long-term perspective and constantly examine and rebalance your portfolio to ensure that it is aligned with your objectives.

Identifying High-Potential Investments

Finding high-potential investments may be a tough undertaking, since there are innumerable investment possibilities accessible, and not all of them are made equal. Yet, by knowing the fundamental characteristics that lead to a successful investment, investors may enhance their odds of selecting high-potential possibilities.

The first aspect to examine when choosing high-potential investments is the underlying fundamentals of the business. For equities, this includes elements like revenue growth, profitability, and competitive advantages. For real estate, this includes criteria such as location, property quality, and potential for rental revenue.

Another key element to examine is the market situation. This covers the larger economic climate, as well as developments unique to the business or sector in which the investment works. For example, if the economy is in a recession, it may be tougher to discover high-potential investments, since many firms may be failing. On the other hand, if a certain sector is undergoing significant expansion, there may be several options for high-potential investments.

Investors should also examine the amount of risk connected with the investment.

Higher-risk investments often provide the potential for bigger profits but also come with a greater possibility for losses. Lower-risk assets, such as bonds or real estate, may give lesser returns but also come with a reduced danger of loss.

Another significant element to consider is the investment timeline. Certain assets, such as equities, may be better suitable for long-term investments, while others, such as real estate or commodities, may be more suited for shorter-term investments.

Lastly, investors should analyze the value of the investment. This covers measures such as the price-to-earnings ratio for stocks or the price-to-rent ratio for real estate. If an investment is overpriced, it may be less likely to deliver large returns in the future.

To find high-potential assets, investors should perform rigorous study and analysis. This might entail studying financial documents, researching market trends, and evaluating the competitive environment. Investors may also consider getting the opinion of a financial expert, who can give further insights and direction.

Selecting high-potential investments needs a mix of criteria, including underlying fundamentals, market circumstances, risk level, investment timeline, and value. By performing rigorous study and analysis and getting the counsel of a financial expert, investors may boost their odds of uncovering high-potential investment opportunities. Remember to always have a long-term perspective and thoroughly consider the risks connected with every investment opportunity

Minimizing Risks and Maximizing Returns

Investment is a crucial component of developing wealth and accomplishing financial objectives. But, with every investment comes a degree of risk. To achieve financial success, it is vital to reduce risks while maximizing profits.

Diversification: One of the major methods to limit risk is via diversity. This entails diversifying your assets among several asset types such as equities, bonds, real estate, commodities, and cash. Diversification helps to decrease risk by minimizing exposure to any one asset type. It is crucial to understand that diversity does not guarantee profits, but it helps lessen the total risk of your investment portfolio.

Asset allocation: Asset allocation is another essential method for reducing risk and optimizing profits. This entails splitting your investment portfolio into several asset classes depending on your risk tolerance and investment objectives. For example, a younger investor with a longer time horizon may have a bigger allocation to equities, whereas an older investor with a shorter time horizon may have a higher allocation to bonds. Asset allocation helps to manage risk and return depending on your investing goals.

Risk assessment: Before investing in any asset, it is vital to consider the risk associated with the investment. This entails examining aspects such as the industry trends, market circumstances, financial performance of the organization, and competitive landscape. It is vital to understand the possible dangers connected with any investment before investing your money.

Regular portfolio review: It is important to regularly review your investment portfolio to ensure that it is aligned with your investment goals and risk tolerance. This involves monitoring the performance of your investments and making adjustments as needed. Regular portfolio review helps to minimize risk by ensuring that your investments are in line with your overall investment strategy.

Professional advice: Seeking the advice of a professional financial advisor can help to minimize risk and maximize returns. A financial advisor can help to identify potential risks in your portfolio and provide guidance on how to manage those risks. They can also help you to identify investment opportunities that align with your investment goals and risk tolerance.

Minimizing risk and maximizing returns requires a combination of strategies such as diversification, asset allocation, risk assessment, regular portfolio review, and seeking the advice of a professional financial advisor. By implementing these strategies, you can reduce the overall risk in your investment portfolio while increasing your chances of achieving your financial goals. Remember to always maintain a long-term perspective and avoid making impulsive investment decisions based on short-term market fluctuations.

CHAPTER FOUR

LEVERAGING TECHNOLOGY AND THE POWER OF THE INTERNET

Exploring Online Business Opportunities

In today's digital world, internet business chances are growing more popular. Establishing an internet company may give flexibility, inexpensive initial expenses, and the potential for significant profitability. Let's consider some of the internet business prospects accessible and how to investigate them.

E-commerce: One of the most popular internet business prospects is e-commerce. This entails selling things or services online via an online shop or marketplace. Establishing an e-commerce company may be relatively straightforward, with platforms like Shopify and WooCommerce giving easy-to-use tools for setting up an online shop. E-commerce gives the chance to reach a huge audience and may be quite lucrative if done properly.

Affiliate marketing: Affiliate marketing includes advertising other firms' goods and receiving a commission for each sale made via your unique affiliate link. This may be done via a website, social media, or email marketing. Affiliate marketing may be a terrific method to monetize your current audience or specialty.

Online courses: Developing and marketing online

courses is another popular internet business possibility. This entails sharing your knowledge or experience on a specific issue and delivering value to your audience. Online courses may be marketed via companies like Udemy or Teachable and can provide a continuing stream of revenue.

Freelancing: Freelancing entails giving services to customers online, such as site design, content development, or virtual assistant services. Sites like Upwork and Fiverr give chances for freelancers to locate customers and expand their companies. Freelancing gives flexibility in terms of workload and may be a wonderful approach to establishing a portfolio of work.

Blogging: Creating a blog is another internet business option. This entails developing material on a certain subject and establishing a following via social media and search engine optimization. After you have acquired a big enough readership, you may monetize your blog via advertising or sponsored content.

While considering online business prospects, it is crucial to examine your talents, hobbies, and market need. Study your selected niche and competitors to guarantee there is a demand for your product or service. Develop a business strategy and establish realistic objectives for your firm. Remember that creating a successful internet company requires time and effort, so be prepared to put in the work.

Internet business prospects present a terrific opportunity to establish a company with cheap overhead expenses and high revenue potential. E-commerce, affiliate marketing, online courses, freelancing, and blogging are just a few examples of online business prospects accessible. While considering online business options, it is crucial to examine your talents, hobbies, and market demand to guarantee you can develop a profitable and sustainable firm.

Monetizing Your Skills and Knowledge Online

In today's digital world, there are numerous ways to monetize your talents and expertise online. From providing online courses to selling coaching services, there are numerous ways to utilize your skills to produce cash. Here are some of the ways you may monetize your talents and expertise online.

Online courses: Developing and marketing online courses is one of the most popular methods to monetize your talents and expertise online. This entails sharing your knowledge on a specific subject and building a course that gives value to your audience. Online courses may be marketed via services like Udemy, Teachable, or your website. You may charge a one-time fee or a monthly subscription for access to your course.

Coaching and consulting: Providing coaching and consulting services is another common strategy to monetize your talents and experience. Coaching comprises offering one-on-one or group coaching sessions to customers who are trying to enhance their abilities or attain certain objectives. You may provide coaching and consulting services using platforms like Zoom, Skype, or your website. You may charge per hour or provide packages for a fixed number of sessions.

Freelancing: Freelancing entails giving services to customers online, such as site design, content development, or virtual assistant services. If you have specialized expertise in these areas, you may utilize freelancing sites like Upwork or Fiverr to acquire customers and expand your company. Freelancing gives flexibility in terms of workload and may be a wonderful approach to establishing a portfolio of work.

Writing and blogging: If you have a flair for writing, you may monetize your abilities by providing material for websites, blogs, or social media platforms. Many organizations and people are prepared to pay for high-quality content that engages their audience. You may even establish your blog and monetize it with advertising or sponsored content.

Digital products: If you have specialized knowledge or expertise in a particular area, you can create digital products like ebooks, templates, or software that provide value to your audience. You may sell your digital items on your website or marketplaces like Gumroad or Etsy.
When selling your talents and expertise online, it is crucial to define your target audience and establish a marketing strategy that targets them. Study your competitors and find what sets you distinct from other services in your niche. Set realistic goals and timelines for your business and track your progress over time.

There are many ways to monetize your skills and knowledge online. Online classes, coaching and consulting, freelancing, writing and blogging, and digital goods are just a few examples of the options accessible. When monetizing your skills and knowledge online, it is important to identify your target audience, create a marketing plan, and set realistic goals for your business. With the appropriate technique, you may transform your talents and expertise into a thriving internet company.

Using Social Media to Build a Brand and Reach Customers

Social media has become a vital part of our everyday lives, with billions of people across the globe utilizing social media platforms every day. It has also become a strong tool for companies to establish their brand and contact new consumers. Here are tips on how companies may utilize social media to develop a brand and contact consumers.

Identify your target audience: The first step to utilizing social media successfully is to establish your target audience. Determine who your potential consumers are, what they are interested in, and how they participate in social media. This will help you develop content that connects with your target audience and reaches them where they are.

Pick the correct platforms: There are various social media platforms accessible, each with its strengths and disadvantages. It is crucial to identify the platforms that are most relevant to your target audience and connect with your company objectives. For example, if you are targeting younger audiences, sites like TikTok or Snapchat may be more beneficial than Facebook.

Create a content plan: After you have defined your target audience and picked the relevant channels, the next step is to establish a content strategy. This requires developing material that is relevant, interesting, and beneficial to your target audience. Your content strategy should also fit with your company objectives and identity.

Create a community: Social media is all about developing relationships and connections. To establish a strong social media presence, you need to connect with your audience and build a community around your company. Reply to comments and messages, distribute user-generated material, and encourage your fans to connect with your company.

Use social media advertising: Social media Advertising is a powerful tool for businesses to reach potential customers. Sites like Facebook, Instagram, and LinkedIn provide tailored advertising solutions that enable you to reach certain demographics and interests. By using social media advertising, you can amplify your reach and increase brand awareness.

Measure and evaluate your outcomes: Lastly, it is crucial to measure and analyze your social media results. This will help you understand what is working and what is not, and make improvements to your plan appropriately. Utilize analytics tools given by social media sites to measure interaction, reach, and conversions.

Social media is a strong tool for companies to create a brand and attract prospective consumers. By identifying your target audience, picking the correct platforms, implementing a content strategy, building a community, leveraging social media advertising, and monitoring your results, you can create a successful social media presence for your company. Social media is an ever-evolving world, so it is crucial to remain up-to-date with the newest trends and best practices to stay ahead of the competition.

CHAPTER FIVE

SCALING UP FOR LONG-TERM WEALTH

Building a Strong Business Foundation

Establishing a solid company foundation is crucial to the long-term success of any firm. It takes meticulous preparation, a thorough grasp of the market and competitors, and the capacity to respond to changing conditions. In developing a good company foundation, consider the following critical factors.

Create a clear vision and mission statement: When establishing any firm, it is necessary to have a clear vision and mission statement. A vision statement sets the long-term aims of the firm, while a mission statement emphasizes its purpose and principles. These statements should be succinct, simple to comprehend and represent the values and ambitions of the organization.

Do market research: Undertaking market research is vital to understanding the market, competitors, and future clients. This research might involve assessing industry trends, examining the competitors, and selecting target consumers. This information may help firms build goods or services that fulfill the demands of their target clients.

Build a strong brand: Establishing a strong brand is key to developing a successful company. A strong brand helps companies separate themselves from the competition and establish a devoted consumer base. This might entail designing a distinctive logo, brand message, and a consistent visual identity across all marketing media.

Create a solid team: Creating a strong team is vital to the success of any organization. This involves employing workers that are talented, motivated, and aligned with the company's beliefs and objectives. Companies should also develop a good work atmosphere that stimulates cooperation, creativity, and innovation.

Develop a financial plan: Developing a financial plan is critical to the success of any business. This plan should include a budget, financial projections, and a plan for managing cash flow. It should also include strategies for raising capital, such as seeking investors or securing loans.

Establish operational processes: Establishing operational processes is critical to ensuring that a business runs smoothly and efficiently. This can include developing standard operating procedures, creating workflows, and using technology to streamline processes.

Stay agile: Finally, businesses need to stay agile and adaptable. The business landscape is constantly changing, and businesses that can adapt quickly to new challenges and opportunities are more likely to succeed in the long term. This may involve pivoting the business strategy, embracing new technology, or adjusting to changes in the market.

Building a strong business foundation requires careful planning, a clear understanding of the market and competition, and the ability to adapt to changing circumstances. By developing a clear vision and mission statement, conducting market research, creating a strong brand, building a solid team, developing a financial plan, establishing operational processes, and staying agile, businesses can create a strong foundation for long-term success.

Creating Multiple Streams of Income

Generating several streams of income is a technique that entails creating revenue from many sources, rather than depending on a single source of income. This technique may give financial stability and flexibility, as well as the opportunity for higher wealth and income development. Here are several fundamental tactics for producing various sources of income.

Start a side hustle: A side hustle is a part-time job or company that may create extra revenue outside of your principal source of income. This might involve freelance employment, consulting, or selling things online. Establishing a side hustle may offer a regular stream of extra money and also provide you the freedom to select your hours and work on your terms.

Invest in real estate: Investing in real estate may offer passive income in the form of rental income, as well as the possibility for a lo-term increase in the property's value. This might involve acquiring rental properties, flipping homes, or investing in real estate investment trusts (REITs) (REITs).

Invest in the stock market: Investing in the stock market may be a source of passive income via dividends and capital gains. This may involve investing in individual equities, mutual funds, or exchange-traded funds (ETFs) (ETFs).

Develop and sell digital items: Producing and selling digital products, such as ebooks, online courses, or software, maybe a source of passive revenue that takes minimum continuous work after the product is generated. This may be done via sites like Amazon, Udemy, or Etsy.

Get royalties: Receiving royalties from creative works, such as books, music, or patents, may give a source of passive income that can continue for years. This might entail licensing your work to publishers, record labels, or other entities.

Engage in the gig economy: Participation in the gig economy, such as driving for Uber or delivering food for DoorDash, may offer a source of extra money on a flexible schedule.

Establish a company: Beginning a business may give a source of income that can increase over time. This may involve beginning a franchise, purchasing an existing firm, or starting a new business from scratch.

In conclusion, generating numerous sources of income may bring financial stability, flexibility, and the opportunity for increased wealth and income development. By starting a side hustle, investing in real estate or the stock market, creating and selling digital products, earning royalties, participating in the gig economy, or starting a business, individuals can create multiple sources of income that can support their financial goals and provide long-term financial stability.

Growing and Scaling Your Business

Expanding and scaling a company means extending the size and scope of the firm to increase revenue, profitability, and market share. To properly build and scale a firm, numerous main tactics may be implemented.

Create a Growth Strategy: To effectively develop and scale a firm, it is vital to have a clear growth plan in place. This entails identifying major growth possibilities, including expanding into new areas, launching new goods or services, or boosting marketing and advertising activities. It is also vital to create clear goals and objectives for development and to build a strategy to accomplish these goals.

Invest in Marketing and Advertising: Good marketing and advertising may assist to boost brand recognition, attract new consumers, and drive sales. This might entail investing in social media marketing, search engine optimization (SEO), pay-per-click (PPC) advertising, or other kinds of digital marketing. It is crucial to evaluate and assess the outcomes of marketing and advertising initiatives to ensure that they are successful in driving growth and providing a good return on investment (ROI) (ROI).

Expand into New Markets: Extending into new markets may assist businesses to grow revenue and profitability by reaching new consumers and tapping into new sources of demand. This might entail entering new geographic markets, targeting new client groups, or expanding into new product or service categories. It is vital to perform market research and establish a thorough grasp of the competitive environment and the requirements and preferences of target consumers to effectively enter new markets.

Improve Operational Efficiency: Increasing operational efficiency may assist to decrease expenses, boost productivity, and improve profitability. This might entail optimizing operations, deploying new technologies or systems, or outsourcing specific services to third-party vendors. It is crucial to periodically assess and optimize operational procedures to ensure that the firm is functioning efficiently and successfully.

Hire and Train Staff: When a company expands, it is vital to employ and train people to meet the increasing workload and expanded scope of the firm. This might entail employing additional personnel, implementing training programs, or outsourcing specific services to third-party companies. It is crucial to emphasize recruiting and training people who are aligned with the company's values and culture, and who have the skills and knowledge required to help the firm develop and prosper.

Establish Good Partnerships: Creating great relationships may assist to extend the reach and capabilities of the organization. This might entail working with other firms or organizations to jointly create and promote new goods or services, or to share resources and experience. It is crucial to find and nurture relationships that are aligned with the company's strategic goals and that have the potential to provide considerable value for the organization.

Developing and scaling a firm involves a clear growth plan, efficient marketing and advertising, expansion into new areas, better operational efficiency, recruiting and training people, and creating solid relationships. By applying these fundamental tactics, firms may effectively develop and scale over time, increasing revenue, profitability, and market share, and attaining long-term success and sustainability.

Celebrating Your Success and Maintaining Financial Freedom

Following 60 days of working towards gaining financial independence, it is crucial to take time to reflect on your accomplishments and enjoy your success. This entails recognizing the progress you have made toward your financial objectives and the hard work and effort that went into accomplishing them.

Celebrating your achievement may take many forms. It might mean rewarding yourself with something special, such as a great meal or a weekend vacation, or it could involve sharing your achievement with friends and family members. It is crucial to take the time to acknowledge and celebrate your successes, as this may assist to generate confidence, motivation, and a feeling of accomplishment.

Yet, obtaining financial independence is not only about celebrating your accomplishment, but also about keeping it over the long term. This demands continual discipline, attention, and dedication to your financial objectives and tactics.

Here are some suggestions for retaining financial freedom:

Adhere to Your Budget: One of the most essential things you can do to keep financial independence is to adhere to your budget. This involves continuing to monitor your income and spending and making changes as required to ensure that you are living within your means.

Avoid Debt: Avoiding debt is also crucial to sustaining financial independence. This entails avoiding taking on additional debt and paying off any current debt as fast as feasible. It is also vital to avoid overspending on credit cards or other types of credit, and to only use credit when required and within your budget.

Continue to Invest: Continuing to invest is also vital for preserving financial independence. This includes continuing to discover high-potential assets, limiting risks and optimizing returns, and diversifying your portfolio to guarantee long-term growth and stability.

Develop Emergency Savings: Creating emergency funds is also vital for sustaining financial independence. This implies saving away a percentage of your salary each month for unexpected costs or emergencies, such as medical bills or auto repairs.

Keep a Good Mindset: Having a positive perspective is also crucial to preserving financial independence. This includes continuing to be motivated, focused, and disciplined in your financial objectives and plans, and avoiding negative self-talk or doubt.

In conclusion, obtaining financial independence is a process that needs hard work, commitment, and discipline. Celebrating your achievement is a vital part of this journey, but it is also crucial to sustain your financial independence over the long term by keeping to your budget, avoiding debt, continuing to invest, accumulating emergency reserves, and having a positive outlook. By adopting these tactics, you may experience long-term financial independence and security, and realize your financial goals and objectives.